GREATEST OF ALL TIME PLAYERS

G.O.A.T. BASKETBALL SMALL FORWARDS

Audrey Stewart

Lerner Publications ◆ Minneapolis

Lerner Publications Company
An imprint of Lerner Publishing Group, Inc.
241 First Avenue North
Minneapolis, MN 55401 USA

For reading levels and more information, look up this title at www.lernerbooks.com.

Main body text set in Aptifer Sans LT Pro.
Typeface provided by Linotype AG.

Library of Congress Cataloging-in-Publication Data

Names: Stewart, Audrey, author.
Title: G.O.A.T. basketball small forwards / Audrey Stewart.
Other titles: Greatest of all time basketball small forwards
Description: Minneapolis, MN : Lerner Publications, [2025] | Series: Greatest of all time players | Includes bibliographical references and index. | Audience: Ages 7–11 | Audience: Grades 2–3 | Summary: "From Sheryl Swoopes to LeBron James, some of basketball's greatest players have been small forwards. Meet the greatest small forwards in basketball history. Compare their stats and careers, and then choose your G.O.A.T.!"—Provided by publisher.
Identifiers: LCCN 2023048815 (print) | LCCN 2023048816 (ebook) | ISBN 9798765625804 (library binding) | ISBN 9798765628768 (paperback) | ISBN 9798765633724 (epub)
Subjects: LCSH: Forwards (Basketball)—United States—Biography—Juvenile literature. | Basketball players—United States—Biography—Juvenile literature.
Classification: LCC GV885.1 .S73 2025 (print) | LCC GV885.1 (ebook) | DDC 796.323—dc23/eng/20231019

LC record available at https://lccn.loc.gov/2023048815
LC ebook record available at https://lccn.loc.gov/2023048816

Manufactured in the United States of America
1 – CG – 7/15/24

TABLE OF CONTENTS

Los Angeles Lakers small forward LeBron James (*bottom*) shoots a long shot during a 2021 game against the Golden State Warriors.

TALENT ON THE COURT

On May 19, 2021, the Los Angeles Lakers played against the Golden State Warriors in a game that would decide their place in the National Basketball Association (NBA) playoffs. It had been a difficult season for Los Angeles. But the Lakers were not ready to let it end.

The Lakers trailed the Warriors for the first three quarters, but they caught up in the fourth quarter. The game was tied 100–100 with one minute left. Lakers small forward LeBron James had missed 26 games that season due to an ankle injury. But he was

FACTS AT A GLANCE

» **KEVIN DURANT** WAS ALREADY 6 FEET (1.8 M) TALL IN MIDDLE SCHOOL.

» **LARRY BIRD** IS ONE OF ESPN'S TOP 50 GREATEST ATHLETES OF THE 20TH CENTURY.

» **LEBRON JAMES** IS THE ALL-TIME LEADING SCORER IN NBA HISTORY.

» **TAMIKA CATCHINGS** AND **SHERYL SWOOPES** HAVE BOTH WON AN OLYMPIC GOLD MEDAL, A NATIONAL COLLEGE CHAMPIONSHIP, A BASKETBALL WORLD CUP, AND A WOMEN'S NATIONAL BASKETBALL ASSOCIATION (WNBA) CHAMPIONSHIP.

playing to win against the Warriors and had already logged 19 points, 10 rebounds, and 10 assists in the game.

As the game clock ran down, James took a three-point shot 34 feet (10.4 m) from the basket. Golden State's Steph Curry tried to block him, but James hit the shot and brought the score to 103–100. James added another rebound, and the Lakers held the

LeBron James

Warriors scoreless for the game's final seconds. Los Angeles won the game and advanced to the Western Conference playoffs.

The role of a small forward is to score and defend near the basket. The best small forwards can also play farther away from the basket. These players must be good at everything.

Los Angeles Clippers small forward Kawhi Leonard (*right*) dribbles around a Phoenix Suns defender.

In her 16 WNBA seasons, small forward Candace Parker (*left*) has averaged 16 points and 8.5 rebounds per game.

They need to dribble, rebound, and shoot from anywhere on the court. They also need to be great defenders who can block shots and steal the ball from the other team. Some players focus on one role or area of the court. But small forwards do it all.

The Boston Celtics drafted Paul Pierce in 1998. He played 19 NBA seasons, most of them with the Celtics. He is their second all-time leading scorer.

One big moment in Pierce's career was during the 2008 playoffs against the Cleveland Cavaliers. He played hard through the entire game. Pierce had 41 points, four rebounds, and five assists. He made 11 out of 12 free throws. But his biggest moment came in the final minutes of the game during a jump ball. Players from both teams raced for the ball, and Pierce dove to the floor. He wrestled the ball away from two players, including superstar LeBron James. The Celtics held on to win the game 97–92.

During his career, Pierce was a 10-time All-Star. He was on four All-NBA Teams, won the 2008 NBA championship, and was an NBA Finals Most Valuable Player (MVP). He became a member of the Pro Basketball Hall of Fame in 2021.

PAUL PIERCE STATS

🏀	Points per Game	19.7
🏀	Rebounds per Game	5.6
🏀	Assists per Game	3.5
🏀	Steals per Game	1.3

JULIUS ERVING

Julius Erving was one of the greatest NBA players of the early 1980s. Many fans consider him one of the best basketball players of all time. *Sports Illustrated* magazine included Erving on its list of the 50 greatest players in NBA history.

Erving started his career in 1971 with the Virginia Squires of the American Basketball Association. When the league became part of the NBA in 1976, Erving joined the

Philadelphia 76ers. He played most of his career with Philadelphia. Erving was a key player for the 76ers from 1976 to 1987. He often went up against other great players, such as Larry Bird. Erving and Bird played against each other in the Eastern Conference Finals in 1980, 1981, 1982, and 1985.

Erving helped make the slam dunk popular with fans. In a 1976 All-Star Game halftime contest, Erving slam-dunked the ball from the free throw line. In 1983, he won the NBA championship with the 76ers. Erving is a seven-time All-NBA player, a four-time MVP, and a 16-time All-Star.

JULIUS ERVING STATS

🏀	Points per Game	24.2
🏀	Rebounds per Game	8.5
🏀	Assists per Game	4.2
🏀	Steals per Game	2

KEVIN DURANT

Kevin Durant was already 6 feet (1.8 m) tall in middle school. He grew taller and better at basketball throughout high school and played one season at the University of Texas. Durant joined the NBA in 2007 with the Seattle SuperSonics.

As a 19-year-old rookie, Durant put up 18 points, five rebounds, and three steals in his first NBA game. In 2008, the SuperSonics moved to Oklahoma City, Oklahoma, and became the Thunder. Durant scored a record 46 points in the 2009 All-Star Rookie Challenge game and led the NBA in scoring from 2009–2010 through 2011–2012. He holds the record for being the youngest scoring champion in NBA history at 21 years old.

In 2016, Durant joined the Golden State Warriors. He won two NBA championships and two Finals MVP awards with the Warriors. Durant played the 2022–2023 season for the Brooklyn Nets and became the 23rd player in NBA history to reach 25,000 points. The 13-time All-Star joined the Phoenix Suns in 2023.

KEVIN DURANT STATS

Points per Game	27.3
Rebounds per Game	7.1
Assists per Game	4.3
Steals per Game	1.1

Stats are accurate through the 2022–2023 NBA season.

ELGIN BAYLOR

Elgin Baylor joined the NBA in 1958. He played for the Minneapolis Lakers for two seasons before the team moved to Los Angeles, California, in 1960. Baylor was best known for his jump shot and rebounding skills. From 1960–1961 through 1962–1963, he averaged 35.7 points per game. In November 1960, Baylor set a then NBA single-game record with 71 points against the New York Knicks. He also had 25 rebounds in that game.

During the 1961–1962 season, Baylor split his time. During the week, he served in the US Army. He played for the Lakers on the weekends. Even though he only played in 48 games that season, he still managed to score more than 1,800 points.

Baylor helped the Lakers reach the NBA Finals eight times throughout his career, but he never won a championship. He retired with the third-most rebounds in NBA history. Baylor joined the Pro Basketball Hall of Fame in 1977. After his retirement from playing, he coached the New Orleans Jazz for five seasons.

ELGIN BAYLOR STATS

🏀	Points per Game	27.4
🏀	Rebounds per Game	13.5
🏀	Assists per Game	4.3
🏀	Free Throw Accuracy	78 percent

SCOTTIE PIPPEN

The Chicago Bulls were unstoppable in the 1990s. Scottie Pippen joined the team in 1987. He played 23 minutes in his first game and scored 10 points. He also had two steals, four assists, and one rebound.

Pippen won six NBA championships with the Bulls. During the 1993–1994 season, Pippen led the Bulls in scoring, assists, and steals. He ranked 11th in the NBA for scoring.

One of Pippen's best moments was during the 1992 NBA Finals against the Portland Trail Blazers. The Bulls led the series three games to two. In Game 6, the Bulls were down in the third quarter by 15 points, 79–64. Pippen scored 11 points in the fourth quarter and helped keep the Trail Blazers to just three points. The Bulls won the game 97–93 and took home their second championship.

SCOTTIE PIPPEN STATS

🏀	Points per Game	16.1
🏀	Rebounds per Game	6.4
🏀	Assists per Game	5.2
🏀	Steals per Game	2

SHERYL SWOOPES

Sheryl Swoopes was one of the first players to join the WNBA. The Houston Comets drafted Swoopes in 1997. She played most of her WNBA career with Houston.

In her first season with the new WNBA, Swoopes helped the Comets win their first title and the first ever WNBA championship. During her career, Swoopes won three WNBA MVP awards and four WNBA championships. She won the Defensive Player of the Year award in 2000, 2002, and 2003. She was also the WNBA's first three-time MVP.

A key moment in Swoopes's career was in 1999. She recorded the WNBA's first triple-double with 14 points, 15 rebounds, and 10 assists in a game. The same year, she became the eighth player in league history to score at least 1,000 career points. Swoopes joined the Pro Basketball Hall of Fame in 2016 and the Women's Basketball Hall of Fame in 2017.

SHERYL SWOOPES STATS

🏀	Points per Game	15
🏀	Rebounds per Game	4.9
🏀	Assists per Game	3.2
🏀	Steals per Game	2

CARMELO ANTHONY

Carmelo Anthony played just one year of college basketball before joining the Denver Nuggets during the 2003 NBA Draft. He led Denver to the playoffs every year from 2004 to 2010. Anthony's best game with the Nuggets was December 10, 2008, against the Minnesota Timberwolves. In the third quarter, he matched the NBA record for points scored in a quarter with 33. He finished with a season-high

45 points, and the Nuggets won the game 116–105.

Anthony joined the New York Knicks in 2011. On January 24, 2014, he scored a career-high 62 points against the Charlotte Bobcats. He set a new Knicks record for points in a game. That same year, he scored an impressive 30 points in the All-Star Game. Anthony joined the Los Angeles Lakers in 2021. He retired in 2023 and ranks ninth in NBA history with 28,289 points.

CARMELO ANTHONY STATS

🏀	Points per Game	22.5
🏀	Rebounds per Game	6.2
🏀	Assists per Game	2.7
🏀	Steals per Game	1

Tamika Catchings had a season-ending knee injury before the 2001 WNBA Draft. But the Indiana Fever picked her anyway. Her college performance and awards made her one of the country's best players. She healed from her knee injury and won the 2002 WNBA Rookie of the Year award.

Catchings's best season came the following year in 2003. She averaged a career-high 19.7 points per game and was on the All-WNBA First Team. In 2005, she scored her 2,000th point, becoming the quickest player in the WNBA to score 2,000. Catchings was also the fastest to 1,000 rebounds, 400 assists, and 300 steals. She won the WNBA MVP award in 2011. She averaged 15.5 points, 7.1 rebounds, 3.5 assists, and two steals per game that season. Catchings is one of only 11 women to win an Olympic gold medal, a college national championship, a WNBA championship, and a Basketball World Cup.

TAMIKA CATCHINGS STATS

🏀	Points per Game	16.1
🏀	Rebounds per Game	7.3
🏀	Assists per Game	3.3
🏀	Steals per Game	2.4

LARRY BIRD

Larry Bird is one of the greatest basketball players of all time. His nickname is Larry Legend. Bird spent his entire career with the Boston Celtics from 1979 to 1992. He averaged 21.3 points and 10.4 rebounds during his first season and earned the Rookie of the Year award. During his career, Bird helped lead the Celtics to five NBA Finals. They won championships in 1981, 1984, and 1986. Bird won the NBA MVP award in 1984, 1985, and 1986.

A highlight for Bird was in a 1985 game against the Atlanta Hawks. He scored a career-high 60 points against the Hawks. But some argue that his best performance was Game 6 of the 1986 NBA Finals. He had 29 points, 12 assists, and 11 rebounds in the win.

Bird is one of the top players in Boston history. He was a 12-time NBA All-Star and made the All-NBA First Team nine times. After he retired from playing, he coached the Indiana Pacers for three seasons.

LARRY BIRD STATS

Points per Game	24.3
Rebounds per Game	10
Assists per Game	6.3
Steals per Game	1.7

LEBRON JAMES

Many fans think that LeBron James is the best basketball player in NBA history. That's why his nickname is King James. His pro career began with the Cleveland Cavaliers in 2003. He has also played for the Miami Heat and Los Angeles Lakers.

James is the NBA's all-time leading scorer and is fourth in career assists. He scored a career-high 61 points on March 3, 2014, in a Heat game against the Charlotte Bobcats. His best performance was during the 2016 NBA Finals. It came in Game 5 between the Cavaliers and the Golden State Warriors. James was close to losing his third straight Finals. But he came through with 41 points, 16 rebounds, seven assists, three steals, and three blocks. James won the Finals MVP award, and the Cavaliers won their first NBA championship.

In the 2022–2023 season, James joined Michael Jordan as the only other player with back-to-back 40-point games at 35 years of age or older. That same season, James became the second player in NBA history to play in at least 19 All-Star Games.

LEBRON JAMES STATS

Points per Game	27.2
Rebounds per Game	7.5
Assists per Game	7.3
Steals per Game	1.5

Stats are accurate through the 2022–2023 NBA season.

EVEN MORE G.O.A.T.

There have been so many amazing small forwards in NBA history. Choosing only 10 is a challenge. Here are 10 others who could have made the G.O.A.T. list.

No. 11	JAMES WORTHY
No. 12	JOHN HAVLICEK
No. 13	CANDACE PARKER
No. 14	ALEX ENGLISH
No. 15	DOMINIQUE WILKINS
No. 16	ELENA DELLE DONNE
No. 17	MAYA MOORE
No. 18	GRANT HILL
No. 19	KAWHI LEONARD
No. 20	CHAMIQUE HOLDSCLAW

YOUR G.O.A.T.

It's your turn to make a G.O.A.T. list about small forwards. Start by doing research. Consider the rankings in this book. Then check out the Learn More section on page 31. Explore the books and websites to learn more about basketball players of the past and present.

You can search online for more information about great players too. Check with a librarian, who may have other resources for you. You might even try reaching out to basketball teams or players to see what they think.

Once you're ready, make your list of the greatest players of all time. Then ask people you know to make G.O.A.T. lists and compare them. Do you have players no one else listed? Are you missing anybody your friends think is important? Talk it over and try to convince them that your list is the G.O.A.T.!

GLOSSARY

assist: a pass from a teammate that leads directly to a score

dribble: to move the ball forward by bouncing it

free throw: an open shot taken from behind a set line

jump ball: a ball put in play by the referee, who throws it up between two opposing players

jump shot: a shot made by jumping into the air and releasing the ball with one or both hands at the peak of the jump

playoffs: a series of games played to decide a champion

rebound: grabbing and controlling the ball after a missed shot

rookie: a first-year player

slam dunk: a shot made by jumping high into the air and throwing the ball down through the basket

steal: when a basketball player takes the ball from an opposing player

triple-double: when a player reaches at least 10 in three different stats categories in a game

LEARN MORE

Basketball Facts for Kids
https://kids.kiddle.co/Basketball

Basketball Terms Explained
https://www.sportsengine.com/basketball/basketball-terms
-explained

Flynn, Brendan. *The Genius Kid's Guide to Pro Basketball*. Mendota Heights, MN: North Star Kids, 2022.

Lowe, Alexander. *G.O.A.T. Basketball Centers*. Minneapolis: Lerner Publications, 2023.

Lowe, Alexander. *G.O.A.T. Basketball Point Guards*. Minneapolis: Lerner Publications, 2023.

Women's National Basketball Association Facts for Kids
https://kids.kiddle.co/Women%27s_National_Basketball
_Association

INDEX

PHOTO ACKNOWLEDGMENTS

Image credits: Kevork Djansezian/Stringer/Getty Images, p.4; Kevork Djansezian/Contributor/Getty Images, p.5; Chris Coduto/Contributor/Getty Images, p.6; Michael Hickey/Contributor/Getty Images, p.7; Streeter Lecka/Staff/Getty Images, p.8; MediaNews Group/Boston Herald via Getty Images/Contributor/Getty Images, p.9; Bettmann/Contributor/Getty Images, p.10; Focus On Sport/Contributor/Getty Images, p.11; Stephen Dunn/Staff/Getty Images, p.12; Matteo Marchi/Contributor/Getty Images, p.13; Bettmann/Contributor/Getty Images, p.14; Bettmann/Contributor/Getty Images, p.15; Focus On Sport/Contributor/Getty Images, p.16; JEFF HAYNES/Contributor/Getty Images, p.17; Houston Chronicle/Hearst Newspapers via Getty Images/Contributor/Getty Images, p.18; Ronald Martinez/Stringer/Getty Images, p.19; Joe Amon/Contributor/Getty Images, p.20; G Fiume/Contributor/Getty Images, p.21; Rob Carr/Staff/Getty Images, p.22; Leon Bennett/Contributor/Getty Images, 23; Focus On Sport/Contributor/Getty Images, p.24; Mitchell Layton/Contributor/Getty Images, p.25; Jason Miller/Contributor/Getty Images, p.26; Ronald Martinez/Staff/Getty Images, p.27

Cover: Ezra Shaw/Staff/Getty Images; Staff/Getty Images; Sean M. Haffey/Staff/Getty Images